D1521308

BLOODWARM

Bloodwarm

Copyright © 2021 by Taylor Byas

Published in the United States of America

Published by Variant Literature Inc

Cover design by Taylor Byas

Table of Contents

For my mother, Robia Byas. It is because of you that I am everything that I am.

My Twitter Feed Becomes Too Much

I come across pictures of two rubber bullets
nestled in a palm, their nose tips black
and rounded like a reporters' foam-covered
mic. The caption reads *These maim, break skin,*
cause blindness. Another photo—a hollow
caved into a woman's scalp, floating hands

in blue gloves dabbing at the spill. An offhand
comment in the replies—*are you sure that rubber bullet*
caused that type of damage?—the question hollowed
of genuine concern. The page refreshes. A black
man melts into a street curb from exhaustion, his skin
blotched with sweat and red. Protester's hands cover

his body, and this is church. A baptism—*cover*
me with the blood. And there are more. Hand-
drawn threats—*shoot the FUCK back.* Police cars skinned
of their lettering and paint from the bullet-
aim of Molotov cocktails in Budweiser bottles. *Black*
Lives Matter markered in thick letters below the hollow

outline of the black power fist. A gas mask's eye-hollows
glinting with tears. The page refreshes. Undercover
cops wearing matching armbands like a gang. A black
army tank crawling through city streets the way a hand
may tip-toe up a thigh. The page refreshes. A bullet
list of places to donate if I can't put my skin

in the game protesting in the streets. The snakeskin
pattern of fires from a bird's-eye view of DC. Hollowed
Target storefronts. The page refreshes. Rubber bullets
pinging a reporter and her crew as they run for cover,
a white woman's reply—*things are getting out of hand*—
punctuated with heart emojis. Protester's shadows blacking

the fiery backdrop of the riots. Badge numbers blacked
over with tape. The page refreshes. A man skinned
by the asphalt when pulled from his car with both hands
up. A police car plowing into a peaceful crowd. The hollow
promises from white friends to "do better"—a cover-
up for how quickly they will bullet

into our inboxes and ask us to hand them the answers. Black
rubber bullets—the page refreshes—a woman's forehead skin
split—page refreshes—a bloody hollow—refresh—take cover.

I Don't Care If Mary Jane Gets Saved Or Not

I can't lie, I tried to imagine myself
in Spiderman's grip—my damsel-in-distress
scream strung through the city like Christmas lights—
I really did. But my black ass would never be

in Spiderman's grip. My "damsel-in-distress"
don't look like Kirsten Dunst or Emma Stone—I looked,
I really did. But my black ass would never be
dainty enough to be rescued by a white hero. The movie villains

don't look like Kirsten Dunst or Emma Stone—I looked—
but the women who terrorize me in real life are
dainty enough to be rescued by a white hero. The movie villains
always come for the white heroine, and she will cry,

but the women who terrorize me in real life are
strategic, hammering out an axe with tears. The playbook goes:
always come for the white heroine and she will cry
wolf. Cry danger. Call the police. The 911 call

strategic, hammering out an axe with tears. The playbook goes—
there is an African-American woman threatening me; cry
wolf; cry *danger,* call the police. The 911 call
a masterclass on acting. Mary Jane would kill me if it was in the script—

There is an African-American woman threatening me—cry
until Spiderman dropped from the sky. The way I play dead,
a masterclass on acting. Mary Jane would kill me if it was in the script,
because what else could I be but the villain

until Spiderman dropped from the sky? The way I play dead
in the cocoon of Spiderman's web, you can tell I've practiced.
Because what else could I be but the villain?
I can't lie. I tried to imagine, myself.

The Black Girl Comes To Dinner

We drive into the belly of Alabama,
where God tweezed the highway's two lanes
down to one, where my stomach
bottoms out on each brakeless fall.

Where God tweezed the highway's two lanes
with heat, a mirage of water shimmers into view then
bottoms out. On each brakeless fall,
I almost tell you what I'm thinking, my mouth brimming

with heat. A mirage of water shimmers into view then
disappears beneath your tires.
I almost tell you what I'm thinking, my mouth brimming
with blues. Muddy Waters' croon

disappears beneath your tires.
I want to say *I'm nervous* beneath a sky brilliant
with blues. Muddy Waters' croon,
the only loving I'm willing to feel right now, the only loving

I want. To say *I'm nervous* beneath a sky brilliant
enough to keep me safe means to face what night brings.
The only loving I'm willing to feel right now, the only loving
that will calm me—I need you to tell me I am

enough. To keep me safe means to face what night brings
to the black girl in a sundown town—
that will calm me. I need you to tell me I am
safe. That they will love me, that the night will not gift fire

to the black girl in a sundown town.
Your grandmother folds me into her arms and I try to feel
safe. That they will love me, that the night will not gift fire
are mantras to repeat as

your grandmother folds me into her arms. And I try to feel
grateful. But *get home before it's too late* and *watch out for the flags*
are mantras to repeat as
we drive into the belly of Alabama.

You're It

—after Tamla Horsford

> *"You are a Black girl, but don't know. you sleep*
> *next to it. crooked bone, split-open head."*
> —Joy Priest, "Nightstick"

The sleepover nettles itself into a frenzy from everyone's restlessness. *You*
sleep yet?—tossed like a horseshoe to snag on the poles of your breaths. The birds are

trilling each other into silence to hear the grass sink its blades into the sole of a
bare foot. The soft crunch of lost battle. Outside, you huddle under the black

tarp of night with the others, shock someone with your body's static. One girl
dares you all into the woods for hide-and-seek. *It will be fun*, she says. But

the thick foliage of the trees chokes out the moonlight. A voice tells you *Don't*
peek as they lead you into the brush, two hands over your eyes. *You know*

how to play right? And sure you do. You close your eyes and count to 30. You
listen until there is no difference from their clumsy skittering and the sleep-

crossed frisking of squirrels overhead. When you open your eyes, you are next
to nothing, night unfolding like a black hibiscus in each direction. You call out to

the group, *Ready or not, here I come*. Taunt yourself with the echo. It
takes a while for the eyes to adjust, to unlearn the shape of a killer from the crooked

branches, to hear anything but the papered leaves snapping like bone
beneath your steps. You are a fawn then, your jelly-legged steps to test the soil, the split-

second freeze when suddenly the girls reappear for a different game, yipping into the
night, open-
mouthed—a flashlight shining into your eyes, your back kissing the ground, a bounty on
your head.

Gas Station

The sky has only started to undim,
its 6 AM complexion
the color of leftover water
in the bathroom
sink after housing
fresh denim, shucking
the blue dye—down this strip
of highway, it is a wound, the chest
of a body
on the operating table,
unfastened.

The Circle K canopy
stashes me away in the
heady tang of gasoline
and white light.
The gasoline pump's hose
gives a small kick
as it retches gas into the tank,
the quiet guzzle like breathing
in the days before death,
the muted caterwaul of expiring.

Then the click of the handle,
me pulling the faux gun
from the hole, and heaviness
in my hands
in the air
as *nigger*
hits my back
quick as a
belt,
and I pull the trigger—
a puddle of gas at my feet,
under my fingernails.

Gasoline sinks into the notches
on my steering wheel
the way makeup burrows down
into my smile lines, feels
slimy for weeks. My hands clean
easily, but everything else
sticks—

that smell,
the soles
of my shoes
soaked

through,
that word like a nude-colored
stain bleached
into a black shirt, splitting me
open like fruit,
or a cloud before rain.

Colour

You notice
a silent game we play
Then   a
straightforward question
                                        unspoken

Jim Crow

'holding   space' on the pavement.

not everybody would do it.
reposition

but the (white) woman   is desperate to
            knee me once   again
    A third time   Strike four.

But wait   this   is

        the standard
                                        this
    denial
                    the
rebellion against

negotiations

I'm

seen as a threat,

I did

not have time to apologise. to politely ask another (white)
woman to excuse

my right

to space I

ain't

free Blackness

never intended to fit

I do not

know

why I know why

No, I don't

Who knew " colour"

would push me and ask me to move.

I have to stand

between

invisible.

A Grocery Store in Alabama

Over the apple bucket, I weigh a Granny
Smith in my hand and thumb the dents for rot.
I check for bruises like these shoppers check
for me—the blackened pit of a golden peach.

***

Another buggy's wheel comes screeching around
the corner, a mother peering through the shocks
of hair escaping from her bun, her toddler
pointing and poking price tags, palming fruits.

***

I wonder what it must be like, no pop
or sting on the hand, no preparation speech—
don't look, don't touch—from a mother trying to save
herself from the pop and sting of not-so-quiet

***

whispers, the manager's backhanded *ma'am*, the absence
of respect. Still—as I grab a pepper, garlic
paste—I can feel these shoppers slow around
me, as if someone paused this tape of my

***

black life, to point to me on screen and say
right there, we got her. I concentrate on the mist
of the veggie sprinkler, water sleeving my arm,
its hiss as soft as a mother's *shush*, or the chafe

***

of a handshake, sliding palms before the hollow
thump on the back, or even the mother bending
to cover her toddler's finger as she points
at me, her susurration—*don't point at that.*

How I Take My Morning Tea

—*for* Atatiana Jefferson and Tamir, Trayvon, Eric, Michael, Botham…

The kettle's whistle is not a whistle, but a mother crying.

a mother crying

This morning's news is soundtrack, background noise;

is soundtrack

another murmur of injustices. My mug tells me "Black

another murder of   black

is beautiful." I lower two bags of Lipton into the water

of

like freight from a ship. The brown color coils from the

freight   brown   coils

leaves like tentacles, like ivy before it swallows the sides

like ivy   swallows

of houses. I add dollops of white. The spoon clinks like

white

half-full champagne flutes kissing, a toast. I have not yet

yet

put on my glasses. The news' main headlines are buzzing

on   the news

white trains across the flat screen, the newscasters' faces

faces

bright clouds in casket-sharp suits—but I've memorized

casket-sharp

the shape of *police…shot…killed*. I burn my upper lip.

the   police   kill   burn

On Being a Black Instructor

My classroom's got a chalkboard, a secret triumph—
the newly opened boxes of chalk, the stalks
like candy cigarettes. Their lost white clumps
flatten themselves against my palms and balk

the creases; I hate myself for feeling relief.
At least my hands can pretend to blend in now,
my fingertips decolored; for a brief
moment, I'm sugared, sweet. Chalk on the brow,

along the jaw, the nose, my neckline's "V,"
I'll write my name to muss it up with my hands,
redact myself—*Miss B* down to *Miss B*—
an erasure I can chalk up as performance.

Then I'll be mirror, I'll be mime, the fox
they lost the trail on, with the ~~perfect~~ hiding spot.

Hypothetically Speaking
—*after* Ashley M. Jones

Let's say we've just ordered appetizers. Let's say
the waitress starfishes
her fingers beneath

her tray for balance, brings brown bread the color
of her skin. Say I over-dip
my wings in ranch

and it drips from my lip, a white fang stringing
down my chin, shirt. Say
I wet my cloth

napkin in your water with lemon to dab at the stain.
Say I only rub it in deeper,
make it worse.

Say the waitress returns to ask—*are you ready to order*—
but is interrupted by the toddler
at the table behind

her, the boy nudging the neon orange eye of his plastic
revolver into her backside. Say
he screams

bang bang with every trigger pull. Let's say we finally
order. Let's say you reach
across the table

to thumb the grease on my mouth, to spread it
like lipgloss. Say our kiss
becomes

a crime scene, the boy murdering you while your breath
is still on my tongue.
Say we pull

apart to find his double-fisted hold on the gun expert-
steady. Say his sausage
fingers fumble

to cock back the hammer, honey mustard now stitched
into the grip-panel's
patchwork.

12

Let's say he then aims at me and fires. Say the empty
clack of the hammer
rebounding

is still heavy enough to jerk me. Say his parents
clap their hands, laughter
sizzling

like the fajitas in their cast-iron boats. Say they watch
me, wait for the clutch,
the gurgle

of blood and spit together. Say they wish for
my last moments.
Say their smiles

begin to strain at the corners, begin to say *go on, play
along*. Say I fist my shirt
in my hands.

Say I spill down the leather booth onto the floor,
right in the aisle. Say
I look off

into the far distance, eyes fluttering closed, then open
again. Say a waiter
steps over me.

Say I reach for the ceiling, my eyes finding yours.
Say you aren't impressed.
Say I then stretch

an arm towards you, rasp out *help*. Let's say you don't.
Let's say you let me die.
Say you look

over at the white family, the parents pointing and cheering,
the boy shooting rounds
of pressurized

air into my black body. Let's say you don't smile when you
suggest—*Maybe someone
should call 911.*

The Titanic Museum in Orlando, FL

I board 1912.
A fake boarding pass renames
me like a new
document, brands a fresh
time of death. No cameras to recall
what I cannot;
the necktie and sock
starched by ocean, a pocket-
watch (a gilded macaroon) balded
of gold flecks, its hands
pegged on salt-annulled hours.
I don't look for myself
in the list of dead, the names
like Star Wars' opening crawl graved
in thin ice, the letters thin
scars. But a plaque wards off
my touch. An iceberg
sweats in another room, and I press
my palm into its face
until it aches, the surface ticketed
with handprints and finger
holes from the guests
that passed before me. But this
is the easy part. On the fake
deck I forget myself—lights pitched
over the railing to parrot
water without breath, waveless,
one of the door's portholes black
as a moonless night—
and catch the hollow
of my own mouth, the surprise
at this sudden rewrite
of history, the reflection of my black
face a stranger
to this ship.

Voicemail to Madam C.J. Walker

Sorry to call so late, but I thought of you
the other day, your history-book picture
stamped into my dream like a president's face
on a twenty and I had to hit you up. Just talk
to you. I've been thinking about your hands,
how they were primed for kinks and curls

since childhood, pricked by the fang-curl
of the cotton bracts. How this gifted you
a love of softness, of running a hand
through cotton pressed to silk. I can picture
your first pass with the hot comb, its hiss-talk
as it steamed through hair and grease, and your face

at the curls' sulfur-cook. And you, tilting the client's face
this way and that in the mirror, their curls
stretched and simmered into submission. Talk
about magic. I must confess, I thought you
were the one who invented the hot-comb. Your picture
next to a short paragraph on my U.S. history hand-

out for Black History Month, your life in shorthand
to keep us black girls from hoping. Let's face
it, the history books are another slavery. No pictures
of black children smiling, no girls playing in their curls
or boys caressing the parentheses of their afros. Even you,
your hair glassed with sheen spray, bone-straight. No talk

of your money, your millions, your mansion. No talk
of being self-made, no family fortune handed
down. No talk of you really living. The books say you
worked in the cotton fields like your parents, your face
deepened by the sun, your 7-year-old feet curling
a path through the stalks. The book has your picture

only a few pages away from slavery, another picture
of bodies pencil-shaded black, and the quick talk
of a whip on their backs. And the scars, never curled
or bent but always drawn as X's by an artist's hand.
And I wish you could have seen my face
when I saw those bloodied backs so close to you

in the book, as if it were all the same. As if the hand
that straightened your curls was the same hand to whip you.
Talk to you soon. Try to picture my face.

Exit 133: Whitestown | Brownsburg

What's dead at night will capture light, the markers
of departure made reflective—a blue and eggshell
bumper disbanded, shards of a windshield glinting
like chromed incisors in the highway. Don't

forget the deer; the jelly-legged thing just learning
to trust the sink of its hooves in soil, the last
car's headlights laser-etched into its eyes,
its insides now out, as sleek as copper plumbing

pipes. To be blinded by light is to scrape by death.
My headlights boomerang to the exit sign's
letters, the Colgate-clean of *Whitestown / Brownsburg*
smiling them back to me—and I notice

the way the words threaten to tangle up
with one another. The way one proposes owner-
ship, and the other, only description. How,
on Google Maps, one is suburbia

(patterns of sister houses powdered white,
their ribbed sides identical shades of khaki),
and the other boasts a shit-stirred river (water
under the bridge). Who punched the letters into

the retroflective sheeting? Was it a white
factory worker that put their back into
the "B"? A black employee cutting the color
of themselves into the tennis-grass-green, the "W"?

Oh, the irony feels different in every mouth;
like a butterfly flitting on the tongue, or a ball
of moistened bread, heavy in the throat.

Pulled Over

I. To the Cop, For Arresting Me

How you doin tonight officer?
No I don't know how fast I was going
officer, I don't believe I was paying attention
to the dashboard. I was singing.

No I don't know how fast I was going
over the limit. Can you see my hands? I'm reaching over to
the dashboard. I was singing
so loud I didn't hear your siren, officer. My backtalk is

over the limit? Can you see my hands? I'm reaching over to
open the door and step out of the vehicle. Why you yelling
so loud? I didn't hear your siren. Officer, my backtalk is
a misunderstanding. I'm just trying to

open the door and step out of the vehicle. Why, you yelling
for backup? Officer, I think there's been
a misunderstanding. I'm just trying to
make it home. Am I under arrest? What are the handcuffs

for? Back up. Officer, I think there's been
a mistake. Can you let me go? My mom gon worry if I don't
make it home. Am I under arrest? What, are the handcuffs
supposed to scare me? Listen, let's just forget this. Chalk this up as

a mistake. Can you let me go? My mom gon worry if I don't
pick up the phone. She's calling right now. And your gun is
supposed to scare me? Listen. Let's just forget this. Chalk this up as
an apology. Officer I'm sorry, don't kill me, I don't want to die.

II. To the Mother, When Your Baby Still Hasn't Made It Home

Pick up the phone, she's calling right now. And your gun is
on the nightstand because daddy died by the blue. His last words
an apology—*Officer I'm sorry, don't kill me, I don't want to die.*
When you hear your daughter's voice you touch the Bible

on the nightstand. Because daddy died by the blue—his last words
on repeat in the mind's playlist—you lose it
when you hear your daughter's voice. You touch the Bible
and only the Lord's name falls from your lips. That old prayer

on repeat in the mind's playlist, you lose it
when a police car pulls behind you
and only the Lord's name falls from your lips. That old prayer
doesn't work here. Before he died, daddy said

When a police car pulls behind you,
get your stuff out of the dashboard. Reaching for things
doesn't work here. Before he died, daddy said
Teach your girl what to do. At the police station, you

get your stuff out of the dashboard, reaching for things
the way you were taught, slowly. Carefully. You hear him again in your mind—
teach your girl what to do. At the police station, you
put on your nice, innocent voice, lay it on

the way you were taught, slowly. Carefully. You hear him again in your mind—
Officer I'm sorry, don't kill me, I don't want to die.
Put on your nice, innocent voice. Lay it on.
How you doin tonight officer?

How Young Boys Survive the Ghetto: 101

—*after* Ghetto Boy, Chicago, Illinois *by Gordon Parks, 1953*

Play house. Climb on a chair of shit-stained paisley
in an alley, avoid the broken bottles. Cut
your momma's housedress, make a cape that's maybe
a size too big. Pose for this camera, strut

like the pimps that limp these streets in zoot suits, caned
and gold-toothed. Know the power of a stuck-out
hip, its demand for respect. Practice your slang,
and call the women *shorties* until you luck out,

get slapped upside the head. Don't turn around.
Don't look behind and see the world's kept going,
that Eldorado dropping down to the ground,
its rims still spinning, pool-hall lights still glowing—

boy look into this lens, let me remember you
like this, carefree, acting a fool like you always do.

October Spell in Indiana

Midnight takes a swig, swallows
        this stretch of I-65 South. My radio

stations begin to overlay like photos
        in a collage—the corners of achy breaky

glued to late-night R&B—failed
        self-tuning. Someone's wished

the stars away. The moon is a crystal ball
        in the cinch of a witch's gloved

hand, my car a captainless flashlight
        sweeping these empty curves

of highway. I'm singing but not really
        singing, blessing myself with muttered

prayer—*Lord cover me*
        in your blood. Let me make it home.

I am tapping morse code onto
        the steering wheel's belly-bend when

dust, no, smoke swarms overhead, a fire
        gutting the sky of a few coats

of black. A car has crashed into the Jersey
        wall, it's front crumpled like a paper

basketball. Fire folds around it
        like the jaws of a Venus flytrap, melts

the paint like acid. As I pass, I see the driver's
        side profile, a black construction-paper-cutout

against amber and sandstone. The flames
        snap like a wishbone pulled between my

two fists in childhood. I cross myself—
        Lord cover me in your blood. Let me—

In the near distance, the Meadow Lake
      windmills rouse from darkness, giant crosses

in their frozen waves. And then *eyes*,
      each windmill's solitary red light blinking

to life at once—proof that this land
      is always sleeping and waking. The driver in front

of me thrusts a pale arm out of their window,
      flicks a still-lit cigarette butt to the cold,

the black and orange of ash and heat
      scuttering beneath my car, searching

for something new to spark. The windmill
      lights come on, go out at once, hundreds

of cameras recording. My prayer gets lost
      in the radio's mangling—

cover me

in ▮ *blood.* ▮

make it home.

Pantoum for Black Boys

—after African Night Market *by Walter Battiss, 1965*

As the sky's colors separate like oil in water,
black men turn blue in the sunset.
Flies hover over the tables,
circle like buzzards: fruit left for dead.

Black men turn blue in the sunset
like cotton dipped in indigo. Police
circle like buzzards, fruit left for dead—
a red smudge on a white sheet.

Like cotton dipped in indigo, police
lights spotlight the streets;
a red smudge on a white sheet
marks the end of childhoods.

Lights spotlight the streets,
but the dark squares of sidewalk
mark the end of childhoods,
and the mothers have nothing

but the dark squares of sidewalk
to blame. We light candles, we pray,
and the mothers have nothing
but an empty room to fill, to lock away,

to blame. We light candles, we pray
for a night without bloodshed, a night that is nothing
but an empty room to fill, to lock away.
I want to be you

for a night. Without bloodshed. A night that is nothing
but a trip to the gas station in a hoodie. Damn,
I want to be you
as the sky's colors separate like oil in water.

Geophagia

"If Mike Espy and the liberal Democrats gain the Senate we will take that first step into a thousand years of darkness."
—from a tweet by Phil Bryant, Governor of Mississippi, 1/2/2020

They say eating the soil might
be good for you. To have your pale
chiclet teeth redlined
by clay, your ocean-clear
mouthwash bloodied when you spit
in the sink. Mistake this for a split
lip, a back-alley beating
that has left the tongue fat enough
to rick your cries for help.
Your grandmother tells you to avoid
the clay cooling in the shade
of the taller trees, and you don't.
After rain, the clay goes garnet, clumps
of wine-dark up to your
elbows, smeared around your lips.
My God, you've gone

cannibal. They say eating the soil
might be good for you
with all its minerals, the blood
that wept from swollen
black toes and dried in the shape
of another country. In death,
someone fed this tree. After a few
mouthfuls tonight, you feel
a little madness creeping in. You watch
the sun set while sitting back
on your heels, its half-step into darkness
packing the world into red
clay. This is blood-warm, the heat
of night closing in like a mob. Bribe
the sun to set on you instead, let
it light you aflame.

ACKNOWLEDGEMENTS

Thank you to the editors and publications who gave first homes to these poems (sometimes in earlier versions):

"My Twitter Feed Becomes Too Much" – *Frontier Poetry*

"I Don't Care if Mary Jane Gets Saved or Not" – *The Chattahoochee Review*

"The Black Girl Comes to Dinner" – *The Shore*

"You're It" – *The Shore*

"Gas Station" – *Soft Punk Magazine*

"Colour" – *Unlost Journal*

"A Grocery Story in Alabama" – *storySouth*

"Hypothetically Speaking" – *Palette Poetry*

"The Titanic Museum in Orlando, FL" – *The Chattahoochee Review*

"Voicemail to Madam C.J. Walker – *Vulcan Historical Review*

"Pulled Over" – *Spork Press (Sporklet)*

"How Young Boys Survive the Ghetto: 101" – *New Ohio Review*

"Pantoum for Black Boys" – *The Journal*

"Geophagia" – *Glass: A Journal of Poetry (Poets Resist)*

I also would like to thank a few very important people who were integral in the creation of this chapbook.

Thank you to my family—in particular, my mother, my brother Jared, and my sister Alexis—for your endless love and support. You breathe life into me. It is your belief in me that carries me onward, that pushes me to keep putting pen to paper.

Thank you to my incredible PhD cohort—Nicholas Molbert, Marianne Chan, and Connor Yeck—for all of our writing sessions, for all of your feedback, for all of our hangouts, for keeping me afloat during this program.

Thank you to my writing friends—Jason B. Crawford, Isaura Ren, Gaia Rajan, and Madeleine Corley—for reading hundreds of drafts, for giving me suggestions, for pulling me out of the trenches of self-doubt, for helping me to stay true to my work, for your love and friendship.

Thank you to Variant Lit and Tyler Pufpaff, for seeing my story and for helping me tell it.

Thank you to all of my inspirations and heroes, to all of the Black women poets who opened the door for me to strut through.

ABOUT THE AUTHOR

Taylor Byas is a Black Chicago native currently living in Cincinnati, Ohio where she is a PhD student and Yates scholar at the University of Cincinnati, and an Assistant Features Editor for The Rumpus. She was the 1st place winner of both the Poetry Super Highway and the Frontier Poetry Award for New Poets Contests. Her work appears or is forthcoming in New Ohio Review, Borderlands Texas Poetry Review, Glass, Iron Horse Literary Review, Hobart, Frontier Poetry, SWWIM, TriQuarterly, and others. She is represented by Rena Rossner of The Deborah Harris Agency.